supply chain

KUHL HOUSE POETS
edited by Mark Levine and Emily Wilson

supply chain

POEMS BY
PIMONE TRIPLETT

UNIVERSITY OF IOWA PRESS   Iowa City

University of Iowa Press, Iowa City 52242
Copyright © 2017 by Pimone Triplett
www.uipress.uiowa.edu
Printed in the United States of America

Design by Barbara Haines

The University of Iowa Press is a member of Green Press Initiative and is committed to preserving natural resources.

Printed on acid-free paper

Library of Congress Cataloging-in-Publication Data
Names: Triplett, Pimone, author.
Title: Supply chain / Pimone Triplett.
Description: Iowa City : University of Iowa Press, [2017] | Series: Kuhl House poets
Identifiers: LCCN 2017005975 | ISBN 978-1-60938-537-8 (pbk) |
ISBN 978-1-60938-538-5 (ebk)
Classification: LCC PS3570.R543 A6 2017 | DDC 811/.54—dc23
LC record available at https://lccn.loc.gov/2017005975

For Lukas and Andrew

CONTENTS

Of what is this house composed if not of the sun,
These houses, these difficult objects . . .

WALLACE STEVENS
"An Ordinary Evening in New Haven"

I.

Round Earth's Corner

Take operation's shimmy all the way back
to the spot where my hand on the fridge handle
unhands whole networks: PG&E pumping

its box-car'd, coal-jumped generators,
the hectic electric lending its bright idea
to last week's Buddha Delight back there

gone bad. I hold the door open till the hum
starts. Cold seeps from the chamber. A shiver
now at the neck. Then closed, then the sidling

miles of cable keeping me connected, the metals
dug, welded, smelted from cooling cores,
bauxite and ore, beat to unairy thinness,

underground passages, new flanged steel.
All that's rolled, snipped, fitted, piped
to reach my unit, me, the paying customer,

heart thumping steady, veins branched
in need of these rivets, bolts, coils, rubber
tubes and tape. The sum trained to wipe neat

in a blink if dinner drips down the white
laminate door when the container spills. If
daily I worship, Power Service, before this coffin-

sized hole of near-freezing I take from, let me be
the thought you think, one synapse among the many
sitting down for this huge plate of food.

The End of Evolution

Say flame arcs through an accident.
Then oxygen's inch, once owned by an oak branch,
gets heaved into the cavern where

a male wed-to-a-wall
blood-trace fathers forth
its big move: the bull in full gallop.

Comes the tribe, single file
down a dirt path between mine
and mine. Or, put another way,

as travel is to travail,
so musings on the moon
as more-than

are to history's
the little zigzag
of singular species.

Meanwhile, a boy says, *Look.*
The millennia—of course—
sassing us much over before

someone thinks to fasten
wheat to a wide plain.
The one time I felt in my hand

the heft of the best stone
notched to a strong stick,
it was good,

like matter sitting down on the front stoop,
                    and thought breezing past,
        shouting I'm home.

        Leading to environment under control,
later given the sack.
        As in sacristy, sacrifice, fissure

                and crack, smudge where the time-snotted
genome of a single goat gets fiddled with,
        making him faint at first wolf's howl

in a signal to save the others.
        Look, the boy says, *an owl.*
                Who doesn't love a too tall tea house

built in a tree for its reminder of the legs'
        vice of falling
even as hands hold the porcelain glazed

        teacups
tenderly to the top? Wavering
                on two forked tree trunks,

        it juts from the builders'
plan like an upper lip
                about to weep. *Look* again

        is what we do,
mother, father, son,
        our six eyes snapping at the picture

        window's curtain of green
for the bird perched on a bare
                topped fir branch.

Needles' hem sharp below,
             backstory and our years together below,
this beast of mottled grays,

                    unblinking, stilled
in the second that is—
        our lines of latitude and long,

        the flatbeds loaded with lumber, clear cuts
ongoing,
        the shipping lanes crammed cargo full—

        nothing like what we'd like
to be by now—
                    a thing that pivots on

our being
                    roped to the house built too high
        and the slow wingspan opening.

Emotional Intelligence

My grammar, 'tis of thee. Sweet
simultaneity when water came down
the hillside in a pipe and a local
Cineplex of Oedipus
argmegeddoned us into a past
no future could agree on. Nation

was another thing to notice,
how shirts and skins, ironies
and their opposite eyed
each other before the big game.
Sneak up, affections. Be covert
in the open. If I sing, I believe

in wire taps bootless on be-
citizened faces, that phat, that
sick: help. We've given up
the romance of weather,
although I once felt so much
for a man who wore oven mitts

in the snow. Land where my fathers
pilgrimmed all we can depend
on, this freedom majestic in
the jest that will what—blah, op-ed
and blather us over, excelsis
deo zapping rust from our names.

The word "to" is understood.
And it's thy placey memories
I love, darling tongue of my tongue,

unique as any finger print
in groove and grubbiness. Always
someone becomes the subject

re-collecting these minutes
meandering like so many sheep
that run before our steps,
and the red or blue X's on their hinds
say who owns them as they go
upslope, in rain, over the stubby grass.

Spieden Island, San Juans Boat Tour, Washington

Among the many mannered spy toys
            rendered to make
                        the viewer less visible

to the viewed—e.g., binocs, mics, mini-
            cams, my high-strung home
                        security system bleeping

in tongues when I drive away—
            the ones I love most
                        are those pricey round owl-eyed

sunglasses
            Jackie O. found for her famous
                        face, a low-tech way

to watch the watchers back
            unwatched.
                        Behind the look of almost eye-

patches awarded the post-op burn victim,
            bivouacked by her life
                        and times and more than,

something there was that widowed a people.
            See now how our tour guide nudges
                        up her nose bridge the neon-green

wrap-arounds of her perspective.
            The mother and son whales
                        are celebrities.

Nikons, iPhones raised to
    follow the animals' scimitar fins
        slicing in tandem through still water:

the mother's
    white on black "eyespot" oval
        alters a pattern I had in mind.

Our leader is called Katherine
    or Kathleen or Kath or Katie or Kay.
        She tells us "it's the Sunglass Hut

mega mogul who owns
    that two mile island across the bay."
        The Frames of Your Life.

"He's a very private person,
    all Humvees with machine guns but," she adds,
        "I'd really like to meet that guy,

one naturalist to another."
    Where are you from? What is your favorite
        part of the country? When I spot three

small black shapes
    on shore, cat-sized, with pointy
        bulbous rumps

like the rear headlights of a vintage
    Cadillac, Kate tells me they're imported
        Japanese mini-deer, brought here

for exotic game hunting, brain-children
    of the island's previous owner,
        John Wayne.

The Duke dreamt of private
      shooting through these archipelagoe'd
            waters

of a western Washington day. Mouflon sheep
      and goats from Ghana,
            equally displaced, make

at dusk the best of
      the island's gritty barren side.
            In *True Grit*, though Wayne

falls from his horse,
      drunk again,
            about hunting he was never wrong,

the asshole. Which America
      do you love the most? Think
            how it seemed to the animals,

my father says on the ferry way back.
      Something there was, a people,
            required.

The deer terrified by this *below-hoof hardness*
      moving not right for so long
            and then rock and sand and sun

bright paining and the feeder
      comes no more.
            In the old movie, it's the fatherless girl

who says, Who knows
      what's in a man's heart?
            Also, glare shellacs

the open oil dribble from our boat
  peacock purple, apple green.
    Put on your dark glasses.

America, which America
  do you hate the most?
    Some animals stay.

Others awayed by men. In the sandy places
  many of our black shapes
    shot down.

Several species have been removed. Hold on
  to railings as you disembark. This way,
    little syllable, this way.

I Dream of Jeannie: Parabolic Lens

A zoom through white latticed windows reveals
his coffee table, her bottle. Past mother of pearl cut-
outs skimming the glassy one-lobed gourd she lives in,
she sleeps lightly astride the pink divan's

silken plumpness. Dreaming, our genie, en-
gendering ingenious edens on set,
circa '70, Hollywood, CA. The boom lowers
slowly, a dream inside the dream

slated for morning, her master. Also what lets
down along this gossamer imaginary:
a coffee pot that pours itself, a spoon
to sweeten his pick-me-up so he need not lift

a finger. Here to look is to labor.
The bowl itself is colorized an over-
boiled pea green that contains the sugar
first extracted by the girl's ancient

brethren, who ground the grains
into a fine powder in what's now Persia.
Inventing as well this same lens
whose arc bends over time to house

the parabola, the parable, the story
that keeps circling back like point A's
love at first sight for point B. Don't blink.
The blonde spun sugar

ponytail coils and twists above her
beautiful head-of-a-pin living room
          Russian dolled inside the bottle inside
the TV box, a homing beacon to millions

     of homes. East meets west by way of
          the tube. This framed square furnished us
the once-upon-a-place called Cape Kennedy,
          dawning in the airspace what was and shall be

a new generation. We as a nation
          "choose go to the moon not because it is easy
but because it is hard." The dog in the capsule
          called "Muttnik" went up, never came down.

          Others came home in bags or missing
arms and legs. A lot of it hazy as your dad
          shoved the screen on its black castors
across the room until even you

     saw and heard the era as a style
ready to be stripped down
          that was. Rest assured, the window-shaped
          rectangle of reflection just hugging

     the buxom bowl is camera and camera only.
If you cut to the one where she winks him back
          to Babylon, taking on a beast stationed
in the desert turns out to mean the giant has plans

          for more torture, starring one tied up hero
and a red hot poker that turns on an eyelash
          into peacock feather, the image sweetened,
          the trick of crystal ball, disappearing.

On the *Nutshells of Unexplained Death* and Other Miniatures

The postage stamp papers
        waiting for letters from the miniscule
writer who never enters make me want
           to eat the scene: a mouth begins

to water. Pebble potatoes,
        thimble sink. The hand-
made cracker sized hearth
          carpet set between the Cape

Cod chair and thumbelina
        staircase isn't enough to close
in on the moment; here
          are the glasses. Ant-gauged

atop the matched-to-a-matchbox
        writing table, so little is so much,
achingly scaled.
          That pinky nail calico

cat whose focus on a pinhead
        yarn ball skews him from seeing
past the one-inch-to-one-foot
          world he lives in

defines me as one who stands
        beside a pencil point and waves.
Think—review the crime scene.
          Dead at the oven door, the little

woman of the house is pinned
        face down to her graph paper
linoleum. Struck or shoved
           or fallen from her mid-morning

work, iron on, ropey mop standing
        careful in a corner. Coroner's
report foregoes how flesh was
           once her tidy decoration over

bone, metatarsal, skull tunnel
        just hours before this last cleanest
cold. Who doesn't murder
        to direct?

Some control mixes its blessings,
        coming down to this cellophane
window blistering
        a wall through which I can see

the mini hero
        laying himself down
beside a single blade of grass,
        if only to enlarge the sky.

Real Estate (the Falconer's Wife Considers the Satellite)

Point of view, which is the realtor's too:
                powers of ten
          plummeting a house

                value till numbers kick the ass of
whatever our local opulence
          has to offer. Dogwood at dusk.

A big so-what
              for these off white
                    kleenex wadded flowers,

waney-edged, upturned
          as supplicants.
I could covet my own mile-high

          scene's toy streets,
              its lawn blobs, blacktop smudges
hugging the dread-locked broccoli trees.

          Such worldly shifts in scale
scale us
          open, making any surface

                dream us inwardly
          all the more so.
Likewise, our mortgage yoked

        to syn-
              chronous orbit tends to say
satellite's

the type-setter here,
hon, its simula-
income marking what measure

can still be called
mine and yours.
Where to house

the annals of
our affections and their opposite?
The mews you built

can be seen from space,
doubles down on shadows,
painterly as some far off pagoda.

It signals,
snapshot and axis upbeaming to one
antenna where the image

is strengthened. Things have the look
of being spied on.
I walk outside,

stand beside the window bars, wave up
in time
to miniaturize

myself,
rended or rendered
in fact, like the hawk

you tried to love
who disappeared herself
into a pine-walled forest forever.

The scratches on your face
      haven't healed. Maybe you know when the right
distance for looking

      rocketed off. Time
           I said I hated the wild
          bird you brought home, I lied. Her eye

was all I envied. Up close she could talon-rip
      into the rabbit's fleshy neck, keep
        that eye unflinching

          which is yellow and no one's
      and owes nothing
         to the seen.

II.

Closet Vision

Holed up behind the whitewashed wooden slats
slung like ribs above the greed-begotten candy plaster-
papered *noworlaters*, holed up and far
from witches in the woods' evergreen fringe,
horse chesnut brews, parents' crow commotion or
robin squabble haranguing the fat
wide open always out there, I read for hours
on the red shag rug hearing market cry
and grave slope, catching the men through ages
of flint and full haggle in my 2 by 6 chamber,
heart bent on Blue Beard, the dead wives'
skeletons cantilevered to a door hook. Later,
hunkering down with amputee hangers,
catalogs, the bottle stash and jug wines,
Jim Beams too hiding with air, no air,
plus a stolen *Joy of Sex* circa 1974,
its pell mell positions and crouching
women, with the POV going scrap and rattle,
some theater of being a little less bright.
Thought I saw one night the million paired eyes
swinging upward, the hand me down generations
spelunking in holes, fine lineaments braved
by way of cream curd and lust and dictatorial DNA,
felt through overhead squib and carpet warp,
some full squat before the slate rock hearths,
more buried in strata of granite, igneous,
limestone, ash, the mind's eye leveled
to one rectangle of light around the animal
who wants to know that it knows and say so,
lumbering down the long path, vanishing.

Recital for Mixed-Race Player

Off key, off color,
disguised as clavichord in cardboard,
            split
level, fretting over something
            forgotten. Beholden
to majors and minors, latter of whom
            could least afford
losing members. Daily followed
            the iron-railed flights,
leading up, leading down,
            with sponsors, frazzled,
doing their best with the mess.
            Sparkling repertoires
of much affection, the bridge-pins
            bought in bulk
for dampening effects.

One afternoon an alleged-
to-be-larger audience arrived, took its place
            in the basement,
children, women, fellow players, all.
            Faces rose underlit,
lovely, a hushed hailing of pedaled
            action, the song
swooning, randy with make-believe
            and erasure. I imagined
they heard the same.

Mistakes occurred.
Then a mild legato in the tune
crashed into the *what*

are you's of *rattatat* and *reach*. Fumbled for
the single chord
expected. Weights above, pressings of pad.
Soon bone-and-knuckle
whole notes, tenderly or in rush,
the timbre uncovering
ivory keys taken from a beast.
Stay back.
Stay confusion, I thought, sinking
inside pound
and pianoforte, the heard, some treble
and bass
that, muddling, made us.

Watching *The King and I* with My Son

As the toy three-inch ebony elephant
hoists his mango wood knobbed proboscis
up and over the empty air above
our set to say *come in,*

his wooden mate, bends as any
good subject might kneel, lessening herself
by degrees. Her elephantine girth ends
in one thumb-sized pate etched, flecked in gold

for luck. *Home.* My arm around my child's
shoulders. Clock, keys, letters on the dresser
where tick pleads the tock and a kind of chronicle
flickers on its throne, offering

altered scale, wanting worship for another
era's place. Once, a message sent "by his blessing
of the highest Superagency of the whole
Universe, The King of Siam," offered

up true beasts of burden, though this
isn't in the movie. War between the States
about to begin. His majesty told
honest Abe back then "since elephants,

being of great size and strength,
can travel through uncleared
woods and matted jungles where no
carriage and cart roads have yet been made . . . ."

She too, made to help, though of small size
and great strength, his Anna, who traveled
across oceans no female had yet graced,
descended the gangplank whistling

a happy getting to know you tune. *You are teacher.*
When lifting her bell curved skirts, each hoop
became a less and lesser equator to cross
on its way toward her hand-span waist,

roping her that much closer in. Afraid,
but holding herself high. Brave, irksome
Anna. Her whisperings like a mosquito's
mini-insistent whine in the King's ear

as he slept on silken banquettes made him
think he dreamt her high electric insect
timbres tumbling: *give me, please, my house.*
He's broken a promise. Now her one thought

of home fills his with the children singing
all day *there's no place like it*
until he's nearly driven out of his mind.
A gold medallion's filigree meddles the beast

of burden's back. Stronger than she looks,
even opulently thin as a gold tendril
still rimming the silk worm's octagonal
chrysalis often is before it gets born

again. One rope tied
many times to a baby elephant's leg
lets it struggle every day
while convincing it forever not to.

Force yoked to the teak log hauled
along the forest floor below
an undercanopy's intact house (give over,
give out, give in) tells us a single mindset

wins in the end no matter how many tons
our mouse-gray beast gains in the flesh.
You are asleep on my chest.
Dearest, stay as long as you can,

your mouse-sized totems assigned
to ward off evil, do. Her wish, a house
to own. In the other tall-to-small tale,
a queen dreams the god-to-be circles

her person three times before entering
her womb as a small white elephant.
Son, the reason you are
is the reason I am still reasoning.

At Wedgewood Boulder with Tallis Scholars

You, rock everlasting near 25th and Pine,
lacking in faith
or clues from the umpteen millennia
spent standing
on the same spot: this week I signed up
to keep
you clean. Have at hand my suds and brushes,
rags,
cans of Goof-Off Graffiti Remover in the same
gray
shade as your surface, the one ablated
many times over
by glacier before the mother bulk moved on.
Hatch marks.
Dents. Large and small striations. Neighbors coming
home.
And when the slow car searching for its turn
swerves
headlights all over your lichen scarred face, I find
the divots
called chatter marks, mossy flecks, gold. There's
the tag
that could be pound sign or face I need to erase,
plus, this
half a spray-painted blue cross has just got to come off.
I scrub,
lisping bristles at the little histories. With my earbuds
plugged in
I can add the choral singers, hope rising from a distant
century

right into this sundown. *In credo*, the human
voices.
Crack open, give it, screams the young crow
astrut
now in someone's mulch and dry grasses
until
the parent black comes back with its cracker.
Here's the give
and get, my aerosol can's *pshtt*, then coat, then arm
sweeping clean,
outwash of this hour *in excelsis* and also that home-
grown girl keeping time,
bobbing along to house music. Flute case light
against
her bare thigh, she's the one I remember
so tiny,
toddler age, stumbling her stubby fingers out
to catch
the as-yet unnamed air. Listen, rock, im-
movable
weight, if in the by and by you'll give
the lie
to us ever having lived, then what? Have brought
for your base
the striped tulips, maiden hair fern, two
bricks
and board for a low bench. I trace
the rough
with my finger tip's small pyramid. *Voca*
me, goes
the singing. The younger crow strikes a bottle to be sure
it's empty,
the child puts her key in the latch.

Another "Scene-Act Ratio" in the Kitchen

1.

Your favorite being the plot of ground
        called motive,
                        making all the edges blur. As after
                supper, the Judas tree
        softens its otherwise barbed-wire
                branches along the fence line.
                        Army green, grays.
                                Bluish recessions where
the waxier leaf sheens leave off and shape
        gets replaced by shadow. Course, dishes
                to rinse, bread crumbs on the empty
        chairs. And if we say the act
                        emblazons the agent, let it be
        not in the name
of our fathers' fathers, but this one, singular,
        standing on my dingy linoleum with his sliver
                of steak needing a container
                        for the thing contained.

2.

He needs to find
        this time the mate, 2x3 tupperware
            never near its match.
        Plastic, marked *do not boil disposable*
(spawning worries,
        the ground, etc.) for the red meat
(spawning worries,
        the cancer, etc.) that's not to be
thrown away (spawning poverty
        as a child recalled).
Because ritual meats from a slain
            beast should be saved.
                The right lid found to cover
the fluorescently lit pore-drilling
        scene, another kitchen night,
            another
                wherethehellisitthistime.
        Getting late, tired. He's had his half
century, opening and closing drawers,
        a prisoner
of war once we don't speak of it,
            the ones he shot, we don't.
        Above the sink, his hands in the window
glass split into
        squares.
        He passes by.
            Passes on.

3.

And if cluttered horizon's another smudge line
    you take to be evidence,
        let X stand for the brittle
            branches. Factor in the tree's namesake,
    one infamous J. Iscariot, who led his own single
successful hanging from its limbs. Leaves,
           heart-shaped, betray
with blunt apex, pinks prolific
      in spring. The Y-splayed
          trunk lets the open pods dangle until
    there is no end of substitutions
in mind, the drift drippingly
        down another
           word run ghosting, *ratio ration rational*
  ir-ear here year and
    yes. Starts up an ache,
this plot of ground at the base, progress. As in
    what was done and left un-,
        the smoke stacks ice caps screen time dry rot
        all the while, that apology
    I kept waiting to
        get or give to the world's
    tallest hotel reverse-avalanching
from a first stick become
    a tool become a
      god.
Why,
    goes the rock pile, a means
        of production, *why why not*
    springs the branch
   of an army, the fighter saying now
    there, there,
        right in front of us all along,
          the cover.

To All the Houseplants I Have Killed

Paper-chapped, heavy fall frost not
banked on. Swerved out the rockery, a brittle
residuum. Hebe, e pluribus unum, liking
brights and light shade, moderate water,
no wet feet. I bring the thing in only
to watch it fail, some second impulse
scraping the land, nakedest, to stress.
Open, you lavender-blue cluster, what's left
of your busy luck. What eco of echoes that
hollows this hearing is: arrest me, item,
or keep your place. Also, the mind, long
enough overlooked, seems less than to leave
your copper burnt curls snagged past the saying.
Mister, bloom where you are: off the box.

Elegy for the Personal Past

Much air-scrubbed the onces were:
upthrown, penny bright, all agape those
instants of ago. Someone called fool's head,
turned tail. Another tried to true the earnings up
until that glitter-blitz'd skyline read
null, new minted *didn't*. Legal tender
came in smidges. Once, I saw the sidewalk
brained and body-slammed, making
the memories more fluxy, suicidal
effigies bearing would be and when.

Now, this kowtow, this through-swerve.
Still unnerves the skid, you see, raws a one
as any rain can disinter a worm. Inveigh
against interim, we must. This tongue a hill
to be taken, never. Each of us starkly changed
beneath a flesh-fall, but several years' toil
enjoyed and, most miracle, this cradlesong
bequeathed. When you think of freedom's
rough abumbling buzz, its siring desire
where we followed every want, wish, wag,
keep a single circle open for sake of
the thing not settled, a dazzle that drags.

Involuntary Commitment with Dandelion
(St. Elizabeth's, Washington DC)

Each criterion must be described.
This one wants, going to seed, the dandelion.
Mother says love's an old man getting lost
in a garden and in the saying we can see him
sitting on the spindly lawn chair clutching
his about-to-be-driven spores, the white globe.
Bristle the cottony spokes.
Synapse, synapse, hold.
Respondent believes he is being watched, overheard
through the weed. To find what, for hours held
up to his face. Spent nebula in there.
Galactic swirl. Fog and star-fluff,
a billion armed privacy fattened on,
barely balanced, the scrawny stem.

who is sick
the one who interdicts

the blown tufts
they can hear us

be careful
an earful

can arm
can harm

the hair if white
is only satellite

A sentence makes shape, enclosure, until.
The flower's rounded tubes at the base,
grainy tassels still hanging, until. Having said,
on first meeting, I am very much in love
with your mother, pay attention, give
what's owed, your gust of wind.

Oh yes the disorderly conduct.
What seems to be the problem, ma'am?
The pounding and screaming at her door,
Buy me those pants
the blue ones I want the blue.
Everyone exhausted,
being watched, listened to,
having to lock the door, count the rising
score and spores in air, the cloud.
The pings sent out by phone, he believes.
Being overhead.

Harrows, again always,
the inner and outer, the narrows and the straits.
Story forth, synapse.

Respondent says you have poisoned his suitcase,
stolen the laptop, vacuumed the data,
impossible to track.

Did you hit her I don't know
Do you live here I don't know

Beware the highway, the fast and slow lanes.

Each criterion must be described

Something overheard.
Fog,
information overload, refuse. Now
I will never live long enough to be
briefed on it all.

The Risperdal
the Exelon the Zyprexa

He says no one's at the center,
I called and called.

Why is the room so white
it's only a tubful
of clouds

who sleeps at the steering wheel
affliction, to feel

who put cuffs on my hands
the giver, the ring of brass

Must be each criterion I am
very much in love nothing ever remains
hidden synapse thy shadow a tyrant
be all the vacuumed data
paying what attention is owed
there are fast lanes slow lanes
as the highway goes who can stand up
volunteer with going to seed
your pound of flesh your gust of wind
with about to be driven spores
I still think of him, she tells me on the phone,
with love and the ideogram for *sincere* appears,
a sun beam falling like a lance
very precisely over the head

III.

Supply Chain

Drippingly by grips, this humus and perlite nearly sings
    through my fingers
circling the ditch lily's heat-sunk side, anthers frayed, fallen.
    Sift. Learn your footprint.
If occasion, rise to. Another bloom, opposite, grows blood
    orange, its splayed
open hand, in shade, still opulent, curls tender, having the time
    of its life.
Let's get the basics, the survey says. Sight says, turning,
    the cat's sprawled
beside the baby rat it found and above the scalp thin lawn
    through the window
the children are watching. Where do you live? What's under your
    roof? What brushes
up, by now, is summer burnt grass in scorch and stubble with
    the rat who will not
move. Lent pallor. Light gray lumpen weight. How many rooms
    do you own? Keep
digging, mom, get to china, they call out, when I work the plant
    free, its dirt
tumbling thick with rooted tendrils reaching. Are you a gadget
    geek, a regular
joe, or technophobe? Plus crumbs, wedged in pine cones,
    tunnels,
earthworm ruts. There's nothing I can't touch here if I want
    to or disturb,
teeming sum of what we're built on, soil damps beside dry
    pockets, clay
at the spade end gone that unctuous apricot yellow. Refine
    your results.

The cat's long patient, knows what her hurt can do.
       She waits, ginger
lines of her fur circling. What's on your plate/
       in your medicine
cabinet/jewelry box/garage? I look closer. The infant rodent
       is trembling.
Another child, not mine, labors deep to find the shine,
       sorting pebbles
through her fingers. Make progress. Take action.
       Witness
not permitted distance. When the prey finally moves,
       jumps a few inches, the cat
closes in, takes the injured flaccid thing into his jaws
       for the kill
and carries it almost like a kitten across the lawn.
       My hand crushes
the dark stamens and the littlest child
       upstairs
at the rat's last squeal, begins to scream *best,*
       best, this
is the best day of my life, and I have to walk back inside.

A Market Storm Speaks

"Why shouldn't I bubble and boom?
My underbelly torques whole horizons
touched by the many-mortgaged, the risers high.

Also, my altrostratus, low
rolling, keeps coming back, proving
cedars in the red, sun leak, worse. Wealth

withdraws. And just what codswallop
got you here? Didn't I surrender my capital,
my privately owned focus? I still have my

to-do list, the laundry and dry cleaning,
outlays and interests, the kerfluffle
of debts paid and un- and how

long did I let the much-rubbed money bristle
over your old assembly lines, Model T's,
silicon valleys, canneries for peach? Once

upon a time, a man said, *I believe.*
Dear Sir, dear key in the lock, who says
your house can't be the house by which we stand,

muttering, *book, pitcher, cupboard, gun,
loaded, on a high shelf*? Pray to me right:
aim cloud bank, brave storm, see index,

trust public, pay attention, take downpour,
blast tumult of billions, read invisible hand,
rub the coin, take me in, dress the wound."

Hungry Ghosts

uncurbed yearning rages outside an answer

with insatiable need we avoid the void

incentive-motivation systems rub raw our

scrawny necks gripping yes yon cassius has a

frantic craving a less-than-self-soothing lean

hungry look small mouth

limbs gaunt the haunt of bellies bloat

the temporary razor slash lacerations

or the one smuggled lemon drop at six

second rituals spat out

your closets overflowing with never worn

gamblers anon blank hoarders

the tags still on with mother pangs

borne by a fetus shed too soon damaged

dopamine empire of work-sex-food-alc-shop-

aholics after our rice wine mouthwash

paint fume heroin attic bulging

boxes of shoes having never touched

concrete outside our serotonin levels

oceanic burnt caramel

scotch assault cedar pine

gasoline molasses old bandages scotch

of near salt-sour quick slap

mouth's back at jawbone and tongue

shoal the hot fisted embrace

down gulley esophagus belly cradle

the brain's all warm bath release relief

where seconds before skull scratched

the mind and towards the end

I burnt the empty bottle's inside

with a match to get the extra drops

A Bullet Speaks

"Came from cartridge to catalyst
each in his cell
claiming freedom

a person a plan a thought a face
facing the crowd concaved like me in my chamber
recalibrating every single second into

the flat nosed entry point
that was a head's parting, piercing its
singular fuckload of lovely moments.

And yes I ripped whomsoever's brain
chiffon of memories
You take any uniquely fragile

lateral region of the neck's crown
its king and saintly cerebellum
and I will rush toward,

if triggered, with my good
old whack-a-mole,
much-intentioned energy,

the so-called kill. No question
metal beats flesh
hands down.

Why not eat a visage if aimed
at upper functions' spun silk infinities
love lust power proven to improve control dissect

because of force equal to its opposite.
After my steel cave
long hibernation comes

the ignition, a ritual
irresistible, his
easy-tear corpus

a trajectory made to be
the victim's last thought, how
I am all the noun there is."

Since My Mother Believes Each Time You Kill a Thing You'll Be Reborn in Its Shape

Swatting the wall's one more
gnat I have to come back as

       Wasn't she right
              salting the sidewalk slug
              till it writhed too much
              how small dose deet for
              woolly aphid just got the cat pukey

As for the wheel in the sky she says
       hello justice, earth turn,   life loan, largest urge

          Or I say, hi there you evermore
homey fact of glutted unignorable globe,
      a rising population coming up from
the male's charming skeetereater
          female's jimminy spinners that can bespeak

a multitude of creatures

Course died under my roof this year countless
house- fruit- and crane-flies
spiders, term- and dust-mites, one feline, a hamster, no humans

Any house houses invisible
resource wars
wood-
water-
air conditioned air variable
interest
rates, fuels
eon-ushered from fossil

those lives proceeding from seed

this peach skin, for instance, bacteria bevy'd,
its rune-y pit of cracked riverlets,
deficits, in the hole,

my would-be
birth canyons   options

this spacious, excitable open

Most days I'd Lysol every crawler
from its cunning, give the least
its comeuppance.

Once hired a guy, *extreme*
discount exterminator
who laid down his mix of mere
mutations

as if I was ok with the one-winged
baseboard scrambling cockroach
jutting up,
body gone all
rust color wrong

as if I shall be
the five legs left off angle,
head abutting seeking
any every corner hungry dark

as if focus
shares a shape
spliced by the many-millioned

planet, my deficit
unlikely to balance my rage,
the proof of our union
the chemical spray's straight line connecting us,

with pit bedragoned beneath the guardrails,
and matter, mater

what a time we had
crouched in a cave both making and un-
by flickerlight

You were not yourself perhaps
bearer and being

Dissembling
resembling

to seem   in utero

how at home   johnthebaptist like   leaping

Shall I sleep-eat in the empty garden again
Mother
munching at zeroes, lipping at roseleaves

for this same space   has both conceived   and brought them forth

Owners of our actions, heirs of

Forgive
the story abstracted
the bets hedged
hobbled by half

my love

come in,   Thou   thorn   although

To the Ego

Be clear as a glass house
ladled in plates, liquid
silica, sand, dolomite, lime,

then tempered, shaped, craned
till you stand fastened
to forest floor, reflecting.

Let the sudden garden strut
up, rising in ribboned slope,
pine and pin oak, laurel,

fleabane, draw markers for
their names, it's all yours, the bits
of talisman and tame.

Also, quit that stupid trembling.
You could be the wild
turkey last season who slammed

the glass again and again, all
gobble and snood, scrimmage
of spit, wattles on fire at first

seeing itself. Be the crash
that comes after crack.
Else, you're nothing but the single

shard that hangs for its moment,
see-through guillotine,
over the broken view.

Census

You come round
        in reading, small
shoulders making

        a certain curve that echoes
the classic skull's
        forget-me-not repose.

Meantime, an underground
        scope spliced into the rehabbed
hedgehog's that-much-less-

        natural home catches the roller-
into-protective-balls for
        the first time on film: its lonely

safer folding into dirt. Grunting
        pig-like when it hunts,
or ruts, like us, hence the name.

        A nest by any other name
births the young up and out,
        mimicking the move from habit

into places where the mind
        may find its calling just as if
a mother's sticks and jerryriggings

        against collapse could help us here,
but how far inside is best to see?
        Take the dark space within

St. Jerome's single empty slipper.
      Tucked below a bench planed smooth
by an ancient master who etched

      him reading the hunched back, set lips,
and minnow darting eyes it takes
      to invent a silence that lets

one human stand for one human.
      That newly-made privacy.
The individual

      funnels far forward
into form, marking X
      to indicate what she considers

herself to be.
      Do I still have to kiss
the demographics,

      pie and bar charts hedging
their one big thing,
      and file exactly right

simply to be chalked up?
      Maybe you need to know something
about the early morning hours

      my mother
once shared
      with a dead man

who lived in the basement.
      His world ended with the saying, Darkness
becomes a light possessing darkness.

Morning she found him hunched over
his tea and toast, she saw him
        first from behind, reading

from the angle of his head
        that he was gone. One less wanting to be
counted, the fluorescent light

        on, green ivy wallpaper printed on.
Paramedics knocked
        him from the chair so that he

crumpled to the floor, making a thing
        she didn't have to see, but did.
Sense us, please, with summary

        file, with population index, by
millions of names per mile, find us
        even by the hairs of the head

that can rise in halo, that are numbered
        in the thousands when a single strand
is enough to stir the sea.

"The End of Evolution" was partly inspired by an article entitled "Is Human Evolution Finally Over?" (Robin McKie, *The Guardian*, 3 February 2002). This poem also references the breeding of fainting goats, as described on *http://weird cooldumb*, July 3, 2012: "The rare Myotonic goat will faint when in a state of panic or fear. Some farmers keep their herds safe from predators by using the fainting goats as their bait. If a wolf or coyote comes to attack a herd of valuable sheep or goats, the myotonic goats faint and provide an easy meal, while the rest of the herd gets away safely. Fainting goats are literally scapegoats." The "Too Tall Tree House" is an art installation designed by architect Terunobu Fujimori. Located in Nagano Prefecture in China, the tree-bound tea house stands precariously perched upon the trunks of two tall timbers.

"On the *Nutshells of Unexplained Death* and Other Miniatures" makes reference to the work of Frances Glessner Lee (1878–1962), an early forensic pioneer who created highly detailed dioramas of crime scenes for use in detective training. I am indebted to the insightful opening essay by Corinne May Botz in her book *The Nutshell Studies of Unexplained Death*, New York: Monacelli, 2004.

"At Wedgewood Boulder with Tallis Scholars" was inspired by the Wedgewood Rock, an erratic glacier near my home which is estimated to be 14,000 years old. Many thanks to Patri Collins for taking me to this spot. The Tallis Scholars are an early modern music ensemble who specialize in performing sacred vocal music a cappella.

"Another 'Scene-Act Ratio' in the Kitchen" references Kenneth Burke's "The Grammar of Motive," as well as James Thurber's short story "A Container for the Thing Contained." Thanks go to Charles LaPorte for drawing my attention to the mythology of the Judas tree. I am also grateful to Devin Beatty and Abby Constable for their astute editorial contributions. This poem is dedicated to the memory of Maury Feld.

"Supply Chain." Several italicized passages are taken from the website www.slaveryfootprint.org, which calculates, based on answers to various questions dealing with what you own, approximately how many slaves work for you in the global marketplace. At the moment, my number is 17.

"Since My Mother Believes . . ." has some phrases in italics from Rilke's notebook entry of February 20, 1914, as noted by Stephen Mitchell in connection to line 53 of the eighth elegy, which reads: "[t]hat multitude of creatures which come from externally exposed seeds have that as their maternal body, that vast sensitive freedom—how much more at home they must feel in it all their lives; in fact they do nothing but leap for joy in their mother's womb, like little John the Baptist, for this same space has both conceived them and brought them forth, and they never leave its security." (*The Selected Poetry of Rainer Maria Rilke*, edited and translated by Stephen Mitchell, Harper and Row, 1989, p. 330.)

I am grateful to the editors and staff of the following journals and anthologies in which several of these poems, sometimes in different versions, have appeared: *American Poetry Review, Copper Nickel, Denver Quarterly, Iowa Review, Ploughshares, Seattle Review, Sugar House,* and *Virginia Quarterly Review.*

"A Market Storm Speaks" was featured in *Starting Today: The First 100 Days,* eds. Arielle Greenberg and Rachel Zucker (Iowa City: University of Iowa, 2010).

"Closet Vision" appeared in the anthology *Seattle: Alive at the Center,* eds. Kathleen Flenniken, David D. Horowitz, and Cody Walker (Portland: Ooligan Press, 2013).

"To the Ego" appeared in the anthology *The World Is Charged: Poetic Engagements with Gerard Manley Hopkins,* eds. Daniel Westover and William Wright with an afterword by Paul Mariani (Clemson, SC: Clemson University Press, 2016).

For their scrupulous devotion and brilliant editorial care, hearty thanks to Mark Levine and Emily Wilson. I am also hugely indebted to Martha Collins for her unflagging faith and meticulous insights. Without the attentions of these particularly gifted poetic ears, this book would be lesser. Thanks also to the many friends and family who sponsored these poems with their lively conversations, support, and loving patience, especially BK Atrostic, Patri Collins, Charles LaPorte, Jill Malat, Colette Moore, Kathleen Perry, Robyn Schiff, Jack Triplett, Parnee Triplett, and my ever-sustaining students at the University of Washington. And as always, to Andrew, first and best reader: *khap khun ka.*